READER I

‘Beautifully written, very moving and revealing.’

‘Very powerful, moving and insightful.’

‘Painfully honest.’

‘Wow! It’s taken me three attempts to finish this as I found it so moving; I’ve been holding back tears each time.’

‘Your encouragement to us as carers to look after ourselves too is crucial advice.’

‘You highlight several key dilemmas we all face with a loved one with dementia: telling the truth or white lies to manage the condition, and the loss of shared memories in the family.’

‘I have just read the whole book and found it very powerful, moving and insightful. Particularly as today as I’m having a difficult day with Mum who is confused and defensive, and I am struggling to find the right approach.’

‘I found your journey painfully honest and because of that very helpful.’

‘You shine a light on the family dynamics that can surface when a loved one has dementia.’

‘You’re so authentic and real, speaking candidly from your heart.’

'Some extremely useful suggestions. The information in your book really resonated.'

'Lots of useful ideas, logically presented. I like the road bumps terminology and advice on how best to approach difficult times.'

'Much of what you have written about extends to many other mental illnesses and those who care for loved ones in altered states. It will not only help others make sense of their own individual journeys, it will soothe them like a beautifully fragrant balm, as it did me while I read it.'

'Thank you for writing this: it has given me much insight into my journey with my sister and her mental illness, and allowed me to let go of a lot of the guilt that I felt at the time and then held on to, as the one who had to manage it, as well as manage my parents through it all.'

'I found myself drawn into your shared journey with your mum's dementia, as you have so beautifully woven rich, universal growth lessons with your personal stories that the reader can't help but connect and be there right with you. At least I know I certainly was.'

'Your book kept my attention the entire way through.'

'As someone who has been on the same journey as you, I laughed and teared up at your stories and your emotional pain, and felt the empowerment and strength of your healing suggestions and guidance.'

'Every detail of your journey together – the heartbreak of her going to the home against her wishes; accepting the new "her"; navigating the emotional ups and downs of that incredible rollercoaster ride – you describe so well the ever-changing landscape of your mom's perspective, your perspective, and how to grow and love from it all. How many people will benefit so much from your book I can't even imagine; I get goosebumps!'

'I especially appreciated the gifts you offered in Part 2.'

'Speaking as one of your readers dealing with a loved one with dementia, your book is so rich in detail about your emotional journey, how you healed and what gifts you took moving forward.'

'I have read your book twice so far from cover to cover, and several times I have zoomed to particular sections.'

'You have masterfully shared your journey, wisdom and guidance on all those emotional triggers.'

'Your book is my reference manual that I refer to when I need to move through emotional pain and grow into a healing place from it. Thanks again for writing this.'

Nick Williams is a bestselling author, leadership guide, coach and mentor who specialises in inspirational leadership. He loves working with individuals in leadership roles to help them flourish and become a source of inspiration to others, and shows how to combine the entrepreneurial, spiritual, people-management and business aspects of ourselves in our work. As a result, his coaching clients have achieved amazing results: landmark hotels, globally successful TV series, pioneering schools, publishing success and influential businesses.

For twenty-one years, Nick was involved with the Alternatives programme in Piccadilly, London, where he met and hosted many of the leading thinkers in the spheres of creative, personal and spiritual development. His own books include the ground-breaking *The Work We Were Born to Do*. He gives talks at events and conferences around the world, and has been invited by many household-name companies to speak to their employees and leadership teams. His work has been featured widely in the media.

To find out more, visit his website:
www.iamnickwilliams.com

OTHER BOOKS BY NICK WILLIAMS:

The Work We Were Born to Do

Unconditional Success

Powerful Beyond Measure

The 12 Principles of the Work We Were Born to Do

How to Be Inspired

Passions into Profits

The Nine Ways to Discover the Work You Were Born To Do and *Become an Inspired Entrepreneur*

The Business You Were Born to Create

The Book You Were Born to Write

Resisting Your Soul

Please Quote Me! Vol. 1: Understanding and Beating Resistance

Pivotal Moments

Please Quote Me! Vol. 2: Being a Powerful and Willing Collaborator with the Mystery of Inspiration

Please Quote Me! Vol. 3: Higher Purpose Leadership – leading from your soul

Please Quote Me! Vol. 4: The Calling You Were Born For – my favourite thoughts on callings, vocations and what you were born to do

Leading with Love: In Conversation with Liz Trubridge

Be Inspired. Be Inspiring. Be Yourself – Your power to enable the best in yourself and others

MUM, ME, WHITE LIES AND TEA

My journey into the heart of dementia

Ten lessons from accompanying
my mum on her journey with dementia

NICK WILLIAMS
author of the bestselling The Work We Were Born to Do

First published in Great Britain in 2019.

Printed and bound in Great Britain by Amazon KDP

ISBN: 978-1-9160498-1-9

CONTENTS

ACKNOWLEDGEMENTS

Firstly, I want to thank Irma Aleshe who became my 'earth angel' at a time when I was struggling the most. Thank you for listening, supporting, coaching, informing and guiding me so gracefully.

My deep gratitude to the staff at the Manor Care Home in Old Windsor for being in the eye of the storm day in and day out, caring for my mum and the other residents. And to Kaye van der Sloot for managing the home and her support.

My partner, Helen, for loving my mum for over twenty years and supporting me on this journey.

To Adriaen Jenkins for being such a helpful and supportive friend and companion to me and Mum for some of this journey.

Louis Cennamo for showing up in my life at a crucial time and sharing his experience with me of his journey with his own mum, and Malcolm Stern for suggesting I reach out to Louis.

Thanks to my cousin Peter Turner for stepping up and taking on LPA when I needed the support.

I am grateful to my friend Liz Galbraith, whose mum also has dementia, for our conversations, your lovely feedback on what I've written, and for our powerful energy work together.

Thanks to Jane Chew, whose mum has dementia too. Thank you for 'nudging' me to take my thoughts and experiences and actually turn them into this book. And for the validation, feedback and encouragement you gave me when you read the first draft.

Thanks Tim Hunwick for gently 'nagging' and encouraging me to finish the book so you could read it.

My gratitude to Adrian Bourne for our precious meetings at the Institute of Directors, and sharing your experiences with your mum and your journey with her dementia, and for your encouragement to get the book finished and available. And thank you for your suggestions when you read the draft.

Thanks to Nikki Richardson for your friendship and energy work.

Thanks to cat Knott for your ongoing friendship and sharing our challenges.

Thanks to Charlie Jordan for our precious conversations on love, friendship and life's challenges.

Thanks to Ailee, Mum's goddaughter, for keeping in touch and sending regular letters to Mum, and to her mum Alison, a lifelong friend.

Thanks to Jill Cox for your wonderful work in supporting people at their end of life and the wisdom you've passed on probably without even realising it.

Amanda, my sister, for all she does for Mum.

INTRODUCTION

I am not sure how long my mum, Pam, has had dementia. After my dad died in 2005, I tried hard to support her as she was obviously devastated. They had known each other for 58 years and been married for 54 years. For a while, much of the focus had been on Dad's health and his gradual decline after being diagnosed with kidney failure and prostate cancer. He lasted unto the age of 85.

Mum carried on living alone in the same house in Egham. In 2011, I started to notice she was asking the same questions over and over again, and I would get irritated with her. I thought she was just becoming more difficult. Another symptom of her decline was her lack of drive to do things. She needed more prompting. She didn't want to cook for herself so much, or go out. Her life shrank even more. But it hadn't dawned on me that she might have dementia. It wasn't until I went to a meeting with her and her local mental health team that dementia was mentioned and then diagnosed, and a new journey began.

She'd managed to look after herself for eight years after Dad's death, and maintained that she could still manage on her own. But on 13 October 2013, I took Mum to a care home that my sister, Amanda, had found – the Manor Care Home in Old Windsor – ostensibly for a few days. Initially, we thought it would be for respite care after she'd experienced a fall at home and I'd spent a night with her at A&E. But she never returned home again. At the time of writing, in autumn 2019, she has been living there for approaching six years and her dementia is pretty advanced now.

It has been, and is still, a heck of a journey. It's been very hard on the heart. Obviously, a loved one with dementia is suffering a lot through the disease as their inner landscape changes. But what is less talked about is the suffering that family and friends experience as a result of losing our loved one to dementia. We find ourselves in strange and unfamiliar territory, usually without a map, often feeling quite bewildered and alone.

In time, friends whose parents have also been diagnosed with dementia began to ask me a few questions, and I shared my experience, which they seemed to find reassuring and validating. However, I am not and don't want to be an expert on dementia. I am also aware that I have not experienced the kind of challenges that you might be experiencing if you are sharing your home with someone who has dementia and doing a lot more of the practical caring, than I actually do.

I am an author, coach and speaker. As I've written 17 books so far, it has felt natural to capture my thoughts and feelings and share them here. This process also enables me to turn the 'grit' of my own life into some kind of 'pearl' for myself and others.

I often feel like I am a deep-sea diver into this human experience of ours, delving into my inner world and then returning to the surface, reporting on what I've found. As I have explained elsewhere, I go through lots of highs and lows, and I have a profound need to make sense of human suffering. I also feel a call to share my personal experiences in the hope that it might make your own journey just a tiny bit easier.

There is so much that can cause us suffering in life – and dementia is high up there. It is a horrible disease. The best way I heard someone describe it is as 'grieving in real time', losing someone we love one memory at a time, one conversation at a time. Losing the person we have known and loved, and finding ourselves dealing with someone different – and having to learn to relate to them in new ways. A long goodbye and a new hello.

I don't remember ever signing up for this journey, but I have chosen to commit to being engaged with it, supporting Mum in her end-of-life journey, and sharing what I can about it in ways that might help others. So that's why I have decided to write this book from a very personal perspective, in the hope and belief that there are some common themes that we all experience when someone we love is going through their journey with dementia.

I have Power of Attorney for Mum, meaning that I am ultimately responsible for her finances, health and well-being. I have made hundreds of visits to her care home – and I have spent tons of her money on her care. I have been through a complete role reversal, from being the child of my mother to taking overall responsibility for my mum's well-being. Not having had children myself, and now in my early sixties, this has been one of the biggest 'growing up' processes in my life to date. It has triggered so many emotions in me, broken me down in some ways while also breaking me open in others.

I have benefited hugely from other people's guidance, wisdom and insights. They have helped me find some peace and equanimity in this journey, and I now wish to pass on some of what I have learned. In these pages, I will simply describe my experience and pull out a few of the lessons I have learned, and am still learning, along the way. I share:

Eleven pivotal moments from the last six years that give a sense of what the journey has been like.

Ten lessons I have learned – and how I have often needed to open up, become more mature, and draw upon greater resourcefulness.

A short booklet that Irma, the activities manager at Mum's care home, and I compiled.

I hope you will find some humour, resonance and comfort in what I share here. And that you will likewise find some gifts, some blessings in your experience too; that you discover how to remain open-hearted and available, as well as establishing clear boundaries, in the face of someone you love and care about having dementia and the emotional upheaval that this can entail.

For me, the journey continues; the sense of resolution evolves.

Nick Williams,
London, October 2019

PART 1
ELEVEN PIVOTAL MOMENTS

I'd like to begin by sharing a few snapshots from my journey with Mum over the last six years.

1. Playing bingo

I had just sat down with Mum at her care home on a Friday afternoon in July 2018, and was really looking forward to our weekly game of bingo, and to being with her. My friend Adriaen had driven me over as I still had **vestibular neuritis**, a balance problem that I couldn't seem to shake off after a bout of flu earlier in the year.

I was glad that Mum was out of her room. I had come to see that if Mum was in her room when I arrived, she was probably lying down and usually miserable. When she was up and with the other residents, there was a good chance she might be in a better mood, and we might have some fun together.

So, there I was, sitting in the middle, Mum to my right and Adriaen to the left, bingo sheets and pencil in hand, anticipating the balls being called.

When John, the husband of Yvonne, another resident, started to call the numbers, Mum turned to me and said, 'I feel like I'm just a nuisance now, no one really cares about me, and I don't really want to be here anymore. Can you just give me a pill so that I can die?' My heart sank.

I said, 'OK, I'll do that in a minute, when we've had tea and finished bingo', hoping she would forget, be distracted or change moods.

But a couple of minutes later she said to me, 'If I asked the staff, do you think that the staff could give me a pill, so I could just go now? I just want to die.

I've had a good life, but I feel like I'm just a nuisance now.'

Then she added, 'My daughter never comes to see me. And my son never comes either.'

This afternoon, those were the parts of her brain cells that were firing. Our conversation continued along these lines for the next 90 minutes. I felt a kind of schizophrenia: my own joy and enthusiasm for life on the one hand, and my mum saying she wanted her life to end on the other.

It was a very familiar conversation, but today it felt even tougher. I couldn't seem to help distract her and shift her mood as I often could, so I felt the familiar feelings of guilt, helplessness and uselessness. I felt conflicted, and I wasn't sure if I should allow myself to enjoy playing bingo or whether to keep talking with Mum. I wanted to enjoy myself when she seemed to be suffering so much. I felt some of the duality I often felt with Mum – to be present with her in her world, whilst staying in my own world at the same time.

On my right, my mum was talking about suicide, as she had for much of my life. Her answer to problems and feelings had often seemed simply to be to want to get out of life, and to die. She wasn't always great at dealing with difficulties, yet here she was at age 87, still alive.

And yet there I was, enjoying getting a line in our bingo game, winning and then sharing the prize chocolate with the other residents, and enjoying the laughter and banter of the care home, which has been a community and a kind of family to me since October 2013. And I also wanted to chat with my friend Adriaen.

Luckily, just as Adriaen and I were about to leave, Mum shifted her mood for a few moments and started talking to Mazel, another resident, laughing happily. She introduced me proudly as her son, even though I had met Mazel hundreds of times already. Then she went back to being depressed again as we were leaving.

Adriaen and I talked about the experience on the drive home to Finchley and I felt a little better. He helped me see that I was doing a good job, and said that, based on his own past experience of working as a nurse in care homes, he believed she was being well looked after. Finally, he reassured me that there was nothing else I could or should have been doing.

2. Entering the care home

The bingo episode was close to five years after Mum entered the home. This is how she got there.

My partner, Helen, and I were away on holiday in North Cyprus in October 2013 when I received a text from my sister to say Mum had gone into hospital. With no further details, I was obviously worried. When Helen and I arrived home, I opened an email in which Amanda explained that Mum was now at home, but someone would be visiting her to discuss whether she should go into respite care for a few days, where they would assess Mum's ability to continue living on her own.

I went straight over to see Mum, and met Carol from the care home. Carol talked things through, and Mum decided to go to the home for a few days to be looked after and assessed. I drove Mum the few miles to the home, and we were shown around and introduced to the staff and other residents.

We went to the room where Mum would be staying and had a cup of tea. As we chatted, I tried to be supportive and encouraged her to stay. But when I got up to go, Mum started to cry and begged me not to leave her. It was one of the most heart-breaking moments of my life. What should I do? Should I cave in and take her with me? Should I drive her back to her own home and stay with her there? That just didn't seem sustainable in the long term.

I could clearly see that she would be much better off where she was now, at least for the time being; if she stayed she might even cross a threshold and start to enjoy living there. But in that moment she didn't want to be in the care home; she wanted to return to her own home. I felt guilty and torn apart, as though I was being cruel to her. It was awful and I feared she would hate me. But in the end I decided to leave without her. It is hugely difficult decision to put someone you love in the care of others. It is actually quite a brave thing to do.

I had a good cry in the car park before I drove home to Finchley. I prayed Mum would be OK and that I wouldn't continue to feel so guilty. It was a pivotal moment in which I had to play the role of parent to my own mother, knowing that she wouldn't necessarily make the best decision for herself. At the same time, I was scared I wasn't making the best decision for her either.

In the end, it turned out to be the right thing to do and Mum only returned to her old home in Egham a couple of times afterwards to sort through her possessions. She moved from respite care to becoming a full-time resident.

Thankfully, after just a few days, she seemed a little happier. She had grown up as one of eight children, so she was used to a big family and lots of people around her. Being in the care home seemed to trigger some good family memories for her. After eight years of living alone, she actually seemed to enjoy the sense of family and community. I felt a great sense of relief!

3. They won't let me see a doctor

During Easter 2016, Mum was having a particularly angry and unhappy phase. I personally didn't experience any physical violence towards me, although I think the staff may have done.

When I visited her, she was lying on her bed, angry because she insisted that her stomach hurt (she does have ulcerative colitis) and they wouldn't let her see a doctor. I doubted that was true, but asked one of the carers, who confirmed a doctor had seen her and couldn't find anything physically wrong with her. But Mum had no memory of being seen by a doctor and felt angry that she was being denied and neglected. She seemed inconsolable. She accused me of just 'dumping' her in a care home and said I didn't care about her at all. I felt hurt but I could see that this was her reality and she didn't want to be persuaded to see things any differently. I also felt powerless – caring for her yet being told I didn't care.

After two hours, and with a heavy heart, I did what I usually did in these sorts of impossible situations – which was to take a break. I decompressed by driving a couple of miles into Egham, having a plate of Singapore noodles at the Magic Wok restaurant, doing some writing, and then returned for round two of my visit to Mum, before heading home to Finchley. Maybe she would have shifted moods, and I might return having regrouped too.

This time, although I had regrouped, she was still in the same mood. As I walked with her to her room, I saw a man writing up some notes at the nurse's station. The nurse explained to me that this was a doctor who had just visited Mum. And he couldn't find anything wrong with her either.

Back in her room, Mum lay on her bed, saying that no one believed she was ill, no one cared and they all thought she was putting it on and refused to let her see a doctor. The doctor had obviously seen her minutes earlier, as he was still writing up her notes. But in her mind, she hadn't seen him and was still being denied a doctor's visit. My heart sank even further.

It was no good fighting her; to try to convince her otherwise would likely cause her to feel even angrier still. She needed to feel she was right. The only thing to do, really, was to join her in *her* reality, even though it wasn't 'the' reality. I remember reading *Nineteen Eighty-Four* by George Orwell as a teenager, and coming across the concept of 'double think', which meant believing in something that you knew was a lie. That's often how I felt with Mum – needing to agree with something I knew not to be true.

For much of my life, Mum had frequently seemed to be in some kind of inner hell, a place of great personal suffering that didn't necessarily appear to be related to what was going on around her. The dementia seemed to exacerbate this at times, and I felt as helpless as ever at drawing her out of her hell, not that it was ever really my job to do so.

Soon after this episode, she was diagnosed with a urinary tract infection – which may have contributed to her feeling even more confused, upset and angry than usual. While it can be easy to put challenging behaviour down to *just* the dementia, there may be other health issues contributing as well, and I have to remember to be careful not to attribute everything to her illness.

4. The 85 phone calls

When Mum moved to the care home, her dementia wasn't actually too bad, but her condition has gradually worsened since then. For the first few years, I arranged for her to have her own telephone line in her room, so my sister and I could call her and she could call us. I enjoyed calling her every morning and every evening to tell her I loved her and see how she was. It was one of the ways that I could show I cared.

Increasingly, though, she would call us to say she wasn't happy and wanted to leave the home, and would we come and take her home.

One day in November 2015, Mum started calling both my sister, Amanda, and I at around 8 a.m., asking us to come and take her home. By the end of the day, we had both received around 85 calls from Mum. Each time, she demanded that I come and take her out of the care home, then angrily slammed down the phone when I said I couldn't do that. To her, each time she made a call, it was the first time she had called. She had no memory of making any of the previous calls.

I managed to handle the first 50 calls reasonably well, but after that, I found them so difficult I crumbled and cried. I didn't know what to do.

I had lunch that day with my friend Louis, whose own mother had died from dementia, and he had helped validate what a challenging journey this was becoming.

As I've mentioned, I had Power of Attorney and was in charge of Mum's finances and provisions for her well-being. When she was still of sound mind, she had said clearly that she wanted to live out her final days at the care home, but of course now she was demanding I take her out. I felt conflicted. Was I forcing her to stay somewhere she didn't want to be? Was I doing the wrong thing? What else could I do? I felt guilty, cruel and so, so sad that it had come to this low point. Should I even help her to die, as she was requesting?

That was obviously an especially painful period. I doubted myself and my decisions about carrying out Mum's wishes. I didn't regret taking on the responsibilities of Power of Attorney, but I hadn't anticipated it would be this difficult. Obviously, I wanted to please Mum and do the best for her. But I felt torn apart, in a no-win situation. So I spoke to friends. I arranged to have a meeting at the care home. I called the Alzheimer Society helpline to seek impartial advice. I joined a local dementia support group in Barnet to get their advice and support, and to hear other people's experiences, which I found reassuring.

The advice I received was that returning to her old home wouldn't give my mum the stimulation, activities and connections she currently had. Also, if she lived by herself, she might tell any carers to leave because she didn't believe she needed them, but if a carer didn't arrive, then Mum would be left alone – and goodness knew what might happen then. Painful at it was, it seemed quite clear that I was making the best decisions for her.

But it was horrible to accept, though, that Mum had lost the mental capacity to understand and act in her own best interests. I had to take charge, even if this sometimes seemed to go against Mum's wishes and she was angry with me.

That was an initiation into a new chapter of growing up and maturing for me. What was 'best' for Mum certainly didn't seem to please her. At times, she even accused me of wanting her to die so I could have my inheritance. That obviously really hurt.

5. My sadness turned to anger

The day after the 85 calls, my sadness had started to turn into anger. I guess I was probably angry at Mum, or more precisely the disease from which she was suffering. However, I couldn't express my anger to her – she had no concept of her behaviour, or its impact on the people around her. What was I supposed to do with this anger, which was really born out of my own helplessness?

Feeling so angry was a challenge to my self-image. I wanted to see myself as the caring son – and to be seen as such. It was uncomfortable for me, but I needed to be kind to myself when I was angry, rather than bury it, deny it or be tough on myself for my rage.

I could see that the care home was doing a pretty good job for Mum and the other residents, but couldn't they see how difficult a journey this was for us relatives too? We were suffering as well. Why didn't they do more for us? They seemed oblivious to our suffering. They became the object of my anger instead.

I emailed Irma, the care home's activities manager, and asked if I could speak with her, and she said, sure, we could sit down and talk on my next visit.

When I visited Mum three days later, she was back to 'normal' and was pleased to see me, had no memory of making any of the calls, and was actually in a relatively good mood for her. That did my head in even more! Had I imagined it all? Was I making a fuss out about something I 'should' have been able to deal with better? Was it my problem that I was taking it all so personally? People with dementia have no idea or memory of where they have been emotionally and behaviourally. Consequently, they often deny what they've done.

6. Coached by Irma – the beginning of a new relationship with Mum

As I finished my visit with Mum, I sat down with Irma in her office. I poured my heart out to her. She listened kindly and compassionately to my difficulties. I tried not to blame her or the care home, and really just let myself be vulnerable and ask for help.

Irma was brilliant. She started to become my 'earth angel', as she was very experienced in the world of dementia. She understood the experience of people who have dementia, and the impact it has on their families and loved ones. She showed great compassion for Mum, Amanda and I. She kindly explained to me more of Mum's internal world. She explained that much of the reasoning mind of someone with dementia is lost, and they get confused, scared, anxious and, as a result, often quite angry. It helped me develop a greater empathy for Mum, her internal world and her experience.

Irma explained to me that, in effect, I had largely lost Mum already. The woman I had known as my mum had mostly gone. I was now dealing with a different person. It was a shock; it seemed so obvious as she said it, but somehow I had been in a kind of denial. It was a lightbulb moment for me. She explained that a significant amount of my lifelong relationship with Mum was over. I was in the process of letting go of the old relationship with the mum I had known all my life and starting to create a new relationship with the woman she was now. I had to start over and learn how to relate to her in new ways.

7. Learning to relate over again

Irma and I had several meetings over the next few weeks. I recorded them and turned them into a short guide, which I am including with her permission at the end of this book.

Irma gently explained that with dementia, Mum really no longer responded to reasoning, and that reasoning could actually trigger more of her anxiety. I should speak in short and clear phrases, rather than long explanations. What she really wanted was to feel loved, safe, accepted and validated. She wanted to hear

'Yes' and that she could have what she was asking for. Irma explained that people with dementia often regress to being more like a child, and are hungry for nurturing, mothering and reassurance. That doesn't mean treating them as children, but understanding they become more child-like. They may respond more to affection and kindness and 'energy' rather than specific words, and how the words are delivered can become more important than the words themselves.

Until that point, when Mum said, 'I want to go home', I would do my best to explain things to her clearly. I would tell her that I had rented out her house to pay towards the care-home fees, and that I would have to give the tenants three month' notice. So yes, she could go home, but not immediately.

Irma explained that this probably freaked Mum out, and made her even more anxious. Mum no longer responded to reasoning and logic. She suggested that the best kind of strategy would be something like, 'Sure, you can go home. Let's have a cup of tea and cake first, and then let's see about taking you home.' This was a strategy of both validation and acceptance, and then of distraction. It was initiation into a new world of 'white lies'. When I tried it, it often worked. Mum felt good and many times, by the time she'd had some tea and cake, she didn't mention going home again.

The lesson of learning to relate in new ways to someone whom we have known maybe all our life is potentially one of the most challenging parts of the dementia journey. Many people struggle with this, as I did.

It was an important part of my journey to realise that being a 'liar' was one of the gifts I could give Mum. It was a way of meeting her emotional needs, although it didn't sit comfortably with me at first, as I am a lover of honesty and of clearly explaining things. But this approach no longer served Mum, or me.

I had been struggling to relate to Mum as her dementia progressed, and Irma helped me see that this was because 'Mum' was no longer available to be related to in the same way. Some changes can be so small and incremental that we don't see the big change that they all add up to in someone we love. And I hadn't really, with Mum. Part of me had put it down to moods that were temporary and which I hoped she would snap out of. But she wasn't coming back. Whilst her physicality remained the same, her mental state and personality were very different. Much of Mum had gone – and I hadn't been able to see and accept it.

I had tried hard to adapt myself because I hadn't clearly seen and accepted the reality of having 'lost' much of Mum already. Instead of trying harder to do what I had always done, I needed to learn new ways to relate to her.

I knew that part of my emotional make-up was to blame myself, believing that if only I could find the right magic formula, I might be able to relieve Mum's suffering. My default position had been to believe that the problem lay with me for not having found a solution or being able to perform miracles. I guess I had a slightly grandiose sense of my own power and importance.

I realised I needed to develop a little more healthy detachment, which wasn't about withdrawing, but allowing myself to be in what I would term 'non-resistance' to Mum and her experience. While, in the past, I'd often had the sense that she was the way she was because of me, in reality her experience had very little to do with me. She was still her own person, as she always had been. Once I understood this, I could be responsive to her yet feel less responsible for her.

And there were also many times when Mum said that she liked the home, that it reminded her of her own family growing up, and when she appeared happy to be there.

8. Enjoying the moments of sweetness – Elvis is in the building

On good days, I would enjoy my visits, and Mum and I would often just sit and hold hands, and smile at each other, even though I often didn't know what to talk to her about anymore. There was so little she was able to remember, hardly any shared history remaining.

She often asked me if I knew her son, and she would explain to me that she had a son like me. I was glad that when she didn't know I was her son, she nevertheless seemed to like whoever she thought I was! And there was a sweetness to our connection, even though, or maybe because, she often didn't remember who I was. She said that she was happy and grateful, had had a good life, and simply didn't want to be around and be a nuisance to anyone. It didn't seem to be so much about mother and son, more soul to soul. Two people with love between them.

Another aspect of the dementia journey is the loss of old 'filters', not knowing what is appropriate to say or express, and what isn't. And losing old inhibitions and judgements.

When I was a child, Mum and Dad had helped to found a Methodist church in Elm Park, Essex, so a lot of my growing up had been around church, some aspects of which I enjoyed, but I also remember their disapproval of things like partying, alcohol and pop music. My memory was that Mum didn't particularly approve of the Beatles and Elvis.

Irma and her brilliant activities team organised a variety of activities pretty much every day, and every few months, Gary the Elvis impersonator would come to perform a set of Elvis songs for the residents. One day in 2017, I visited when I knew Gary was performing and I was amazed how we were able to get Mum up to dance and sing along to songs I didn't even know she knew, enjoying the very performer that I remember her disapproving of when I was a child.

I was constantly amazed at the aspects of her mind that did remain intact, and could be drawn out. On another day, Mum was lying in bed, saying she was just a nuisance, and then Ann, one of the activities team, came into her room and prompted her so that she started knitting! Although her short-term memory was terrible, some part of her mind remembered as clear as a bell how to knit, even while she would be saying she couldn't do it. And she would go on to knit a perfect square without missing a stitch. And she could always remember that she was one of eight children, that she won a scholarship to the Sir William Perkins School, and that her mum took her tap dancing.

Back to Elvis for a moment. Gary performed at many of the local care homes and when his mum needed to move into a care home, he chose The Manor for her too, which I found reassuring.

9. Her 88th birthday

For Mum's 88th birthday on 24 September 2018, I visited her with my friend Adriaen, with a balloon, presents and flowers. Apparently, she'd had a good morning and had been in a good mood earlier when my sister visited, but by the time we arrived, she was depressed and just kept asking for a pill so that she could die. She didn't want to live any more. She would get angry that we wouldn't give her a pill. She kept saying that she was a nuisance and no one wanted her.

Adriaen was a trained nurse and he and Kylie, one of the carers, and I spent our entire visit trying to cheer her up. But none of us could do it. Although I felt disheartened, somehow, I also felt a little validated. If Adriaen as a trained dementia nurse and Kylie as a very experienced carer couldn't soothe her or console her, or help shift her mood either, I needn't feel quite so bad! I was able to let go of the idea that there must be some magic technique that I hadn't discovered yet. It just was this tough, for all of us.

That day, Mum seemed full of self-loathing, completely engrossed in her own thoughts and unreachable. Nothing we could say would stick or engage. She was 'right': she was a nuisance, no one wanted her, and we were being cruel to her because we wouldn't give her a pill so she could die. Even when she'd had her normal medication, a moment later she demanded her pills and denied that she had been given any. It was a bit of a hopeless experience. She was suffering and there was nothing we could do to shift her.

I guess the bottom line, though, is that I was able to feel a bit less of a failure afterwards.

10. Losing Adriaen

My friend Adriaen had taken me to see Mum about twenty times, getting to know her and the staff at the home as well. However, just before Easter 2019, he went off the radar. He wasn't responding to calls, and mutual friends hadn't heard from him for a few days. We were due meet at his home, and I hoped he would be there when I arrived, but there was no reply. He could be flaky, but this was unusual even for him. So the next day, I spoke to friends and a missing person's charity. I decided to call the police and report him missing. Within minutes, the police arrived at our front door. They explained they would go around to his flat and tell us if they found anything. Three hours later, one of them returned and suggested we sit down. He explained that they had broken in to the flat and found Adriaen lying dead on his living-room floor. He might have been there for a couple of days.

I was shocked. Adriaen had been vulnerable after his husband, Michael, had died of cancer eighteen months earlier. Michael was a strong character, and Adriaen was a bit lost without him. He hadn't renewed his nursing licence so he could focus on caring for Michael at his end of life, but then had trouble getting his licence back and lost two jobs that he was offered.

I was in grief, for a number of reasons; above all, the loss of a close friend, but also because I felt I had lost an important connection with Mum and the care home. Other than my partner, Helen, Adriaen had shared most of the recent journey with me. As an experienced nurse, he had given me suggestions about how to enhance Mum's care and repeatedly told me what a good job he thought I was doing in these difficult circumstances. Burdens are much heavier when they are carried alone and he had helped lighten the load. I will always be grateful to him and all that he did to offer support to Mum, to me and other friends in need, even when he was himself grieving. At the coroner's inquest in October 2019, an open verdict was returned on how he died.

11. Celebrating with a song and a dance!

After a series of reasonably good visits, I arrived on 20 September 2019, a few days before her 89th birthday, to find Mum lying on her bed, talking to herself and pleading with God to let her die. My heart sank, and I assumed I was in for 90 minutes of listening to her unhappiness. Often I would just resign myself to the visit consisting of this.

There was an activity going on downstairs and I asked Mum if she would like to go down and join her friends. She was adamant that she didn't want to see anyone. But I gently kept suggesting it and after about 20 minutes she agreed to come downstairs with me, which I knew was no guarantee that she actually would. I kept reassuring her that if she wasn't enjoying herself, I would bring her straight back up.

We did get downstairs, and I managed to lead her gently into the lounge, where she refused to join in with the singing and dancing. But I continued to encourage her, and we started to sing and we started to dance. And for ten minutes we had some real joy together, even if she didn't know who I was!

It felt like a triumph. I was able to be gentle and patient with her, not getting cross or irritated. I drew on reserves of patience I didn't know I possessed, and it led to a different result. I took a couple of minutes to bask in the praise of the staff, who asked me how I'd managed it, as they had tried to get her downstairs unsuccessfully earlier on. I know I am only there one day out of many, but it felt like a little victory to celebrate!

When the songs were over she lapsed back into wanting a pill so she could die, but for ten minutes her happier self came to the surface.

Just some key moments

These eleven stories represent a microcosm of my hundreds of visits to see Mum over the last few years. There are still many moments of sweetness. It still gladdens my heart on the days when there is a smile of recognition from her as she sees me arrive.

Other days, she is just angry, doesn't say hello and immediately demands either that I take her home or give her a pill so she can die, and then tells me I am not helping her at all.

It's still a rollercoaster, and I still don't know which Mum I am going to find when I turn up.

In the second part of this book, I'm going to share how these experiences have affected me and caused me to grow. After six years, I have reached a degree of equanimity with the situation, but still feel upset when I have a run of good visits and then find Mum in one of her angry and depressed moods.

Here is what I have learned, and am still learning.

PART 2

TEN GIFTS HIDDEN IN THE CHALLENGES

As I said at the beginning of this book, I am someone who tries not to shy away from the grit of life, in the hope and belief that the grit holds the potential for the pearl. Suffering can – as can joy – be the alchemical birthplace of wisdom.

So, strange as it may sound, this journey with Mum – painful as it has been and it often still is – has also bestowed some gifts on me. Or more precisely, drawn qualities out of me that had been latent or dormant. It has been the cause of alchemical changes within me.

The gifts appear strangely wrapped, but it is part of my psychological make-up to want to explore what each gift on offer might be, even in the most difficult of situations. Sometimes it may take me years to see and unwrap the gift, and sometimes I don't find the gift at all, but that doesn't stop me searching!

All the gifts of this particular journey fit under the loose heading of 'Emotional Maturity'. The major emotions that I experience, and which friends in similar situations tell me they experience too, are: helplessness, frustration, guilt and occasional relief.

My development into full adulthood is ongoing and seems to have lagged decades behind my official markers of maturity. I know I am not alone in that. During this journey with Mum, so many echoes of my own childhood have been sounded, so many chords struck, my heart has been opened and old pains and hurts have risen unbidden to the surface, while disappointments are re-experienced. So many feelings have been triggered.

When I was a child, I perceived myself as being full of flaws and faults, barely able to see anything good about myself at all. A theme of my family seemed to be attempting to put a lid on feelings, and dealing with them by not dealing with them. Only certain feelings were acceptable, and I was often ashamed of my feelings, seeing them as weak. Indeed, shame seemed to be a prevalent emotion in our household, and Mum often used shame to control my sister and me. I was afraid of my feelings because I had learned they were unacceptable. So I tried to control and then bury them. Up to my late twenties, one of the ways I dealt with my feelings was simply to drink a lot of alcohol.

A significant part of my adulthood has been the journey to allow, process and integrate feelings that I had buried away for decades. As a result, I've aimed to find some resolution. I have needed to learn how to handle my own feelings with a maturity that often seemed missing from my repertoire.

There was a lot of blame in my family. 'It's your fault I am feeling like this' was a big theme. I grew up thinking that if I had been different, then maybe they would have been different. Somehow it was all my fault. So another part of my maturing has been not to blame anyone else for events, or even myself, but to be able to say, 'These are my feelings. Only I can do anything about them.' I have the power to accept them and make friends with them.

So what have been the gifts under this umbrella of maturing emotionally? I would put them roughly under these headings:

1. Treasure your sense of humour.
2. Discover a patience you didn't know you had.
3. Finding emotional maturity.
4. Increase your willingness to take responsibility.
5. Grieve well.
6. Handling guilt.
7. Caring for yourself.
8. Drawing out the essence.
9. Handling family dynamics.
10. Getting beyond emotional inheritance.

1. Treasure your sense of humour

On his death bed, my dad told me, 'If you can make other people laugh as you much as you do me, you'll go a long way!' My dad and I laughed a lot. Even in the weeks up to his death, he would close his eyes and pretend to be dead. Then he would open his eyes, laugh and say, 'Just joking, still here!' Yet he and I had our challenges. Dad's own father had been away during the First World War, and died when my dad was just six, so my dad never really had a strong father figure himself and wasn't able to provide much of one for me. Our way of connecting was quite childlike, through comedy and laughter. He was a playmate rather than a strong, masculine, protective presence.

Tragedy and comedy can be very close. I was recently listening to an interview with the comic writer Ben Elton about his book *Identity Crisis,* and he made a remark I found powerful. He said, 'The ability to look at the endless horror and the conditions that haunt us all and find the humour is possibly unique to us as humans.'

It brought home to me that while our journey with our loved one with dementia can be full of difficulty, tragedy and challenge, it is also important for our sanity and mental health that we allow ourselves to find some humour any place we can. We may not able laugh with them, and I am not suggesting we laugh at them, but to be able to laugh at this human condition that we share is important, I believe.

Learning to relate with our loved one in new ways can be a great source of humour. When I was chatting to the daughter of one of the other residents, she told me, 'My 85-year old mum often asks me whether she was popular with men and how much she had enjoyed sex!' With dementia, inhibitions can shrink, and personalities do change. Several friends have told me that their loved one has lost elements of nastiness while a sweetness comes to the surface.

Mum is not overly renowned for her sense of humour, and can be quite serious and dramatic. Over the years, she's often complained that she isn't taken seriously and nobody cares about her – and the dementia seems to heighten her distress and anxiety.

One way I've tried to create some fun around my visits has been to see how long I need to leave her for before she forgets I've been there already, and thinks I've just arrived. Turns out that these days, it's about the length of a trip to the bathroom.

So, on a good day, I get to be a hero several times.

Her face lights up each time I 'arrive' back from the loo. She tells me how lovely it is to see me, and introduces me to people as her son, and the staff play along too. I joke and say I'm really her toy boy, and she might look outraged for a moment and then we'll all laugh. Then I tell her (again) how well she looks and how her hair looks lovely. I hold her hand and tell her that her nails are nicely manicured, and she tells me how she does her own hair and nails (she doesn't), so I say what a good job she does of looking after herself.

It is a joy to have those rituals, those moments of love and laughter, often several times each time I visit. When she's gone, those are the memories I will treasure.

2. Discover a patience you didn't know you had

One of the big challenges around people with dementia is how they often repeat the same conversations, or ask the same questions over and over again. In their inner world, they literally have no idea that they have asked the same question moments before, so if you get frustrated, they might then get upset. They can't understand what the problem is: they are simply showing an interest in you and can't understand any frustration you might have.

And things can change in an instant. I've described earlier how, on one visit with Mum, over a period of 15 minutes or so, I asked her six times if she would like to leave her room and come downstairs to the lounge and join in with singing, and she refused six times. As far as I know, she wasn't aware of me having asked her a few moments before. Then, on the seventh suggestion something shifted, she said yes, and I managed to get her to join in with the singing and dancing for a while – and we had a lovely time. But it's tricky knowing the line between patient persistence and bullying. I guess it comes down to the energy behind what you suggest, whether it's love or irritation. And the paradox is that the less irritated you are, the more likely your loved one is to be responsive.

Have you got a girlfriend?

One of the questions Mum would frequently ask me, often several dozen times during a visit, is 'Have you got a girlfriend?' I have been with Helen for 23 years now, and Mum once knew her very well, and we all spent lots of happy times together. But Mum now has no memory of her, so I would show her pictures of Helen on my phone. Sometimes she would vaguely remember her, other times not. But I came to realise that what she was probably also asking me was, 'Are you happy?' In her mind, if I had a partner, then I would be happy. I guess she might also be wanting reassurance that I would be OK after she died, as I would have someone to love me and care about me. I reassured her that I did. I think it was also my way of letting Mum know in turn that she had done a good of mothering me, and that she was a success as a parent. (Especially as I certainly hadn't felt like that growing up. Nothing that a few decades of therapy couldn't put right!)

Have you come to take me home?

One of the questions that lay hardest on my heart was when Mum would ask, 'Have you come to take me home?' My heart would sink and I would feel guilty because I knew if I said, 'No!' she was likely to get angry and I didn't enjoy having to deal with that. So over time, I learned again to 'lie' and to tell her, 'Yes, I've come to take you home. Let's have a cup of tea and a piece of cake, and then let's take it from there.' I would blatantly lie in the hope and knowledge that she would usually forget that she wanted to go home, and would stop asking. Mostly it worked, but sometimes it didn't.

It certainly got me being creative. How patient could I become? How many ways could I answer the same question, in slightly different ways? And how could I find the humour in it?

Wanting to go home is quite usual for those with dementia, but it often doesn't mean their old physical home. It is more a feeling of safety, of things being OK, maybe of being loved and nurtured. When I asked Mum what home meant to her, it was rarely the physical place where she'd lived. She had no memory of where she lived before the care home. Maybe it is also the desire to also get away from some parts of her experience that she is finding unpleasant. Maybe, for her, it's a desire to go home to Heaven, back to God.

Do I know you?

More recently, Mum has spent whole visits repeatedly asking me, 'Do I know you?' I must look familiar to her, but she often doesn't recognise me as her son.

Dealing with difficult conversations

Even before her dementia, Mum has always had (it seemed to me) a need to be right. I would often feel defeated and helpless, so would end up in a fight with her and would want to tell her why she was wrong. I took her no to mean no.

Her insistence about how things are has increased with her dementia; that is part of the disease, for example, she'll be:

- adamant she hasn't been given any food while holding a slice of toast;
- adamant that her son never comes to see her while I sit holding her hand;
- adamant she is on her own and no one cares about her, when she is surrounded by people who care;

- adamant she doesn't want to dance and then thirty seconds later beaming as she dances and has a lovely time – at least for a while.

Understanding needs and what is really being said

Another element of patience is having the willingness and skilfulness to understand what your loved one's needs are, which they may well not be able to express clearly. I often had trouble understanding what Mum was really saying. Even before the dementia, I found she would often speak tangentially rather than directly. She once said to me, 'I think computers have ruined the lives of many ordinary people.' A friend later translated that as maybe meaning, 'I don't think she likes you spending time on your laptop computer when you visit her!' She was actually asking me to pay her attention.

I wish Mum had come with an instruction and translation manual! It can take a lot of patience to understand your loved ones' needs. And I know that is part of the human condition as a whole – communicating clearly and effectively with each other is difficult enough, without adding dementia to the equation.

Anxiety

Another dimension is that people with dementia are often operating from a place of inner anxiety and fearfulness. Mum has frequently been afraid of getting things wrong, being told off or punished. These traits have always been in her but are often exacerbated now she has dementia.

It takes a lot of love, patience and compassion to deal with anxiety, especially when it often bears no relation to the reality of a situation, yet cannot always be easily rationalised or soothed away.

At Mum's care home, at the end of an activity on the ground floor, residents would gradually be taken back up to the first floor where they would have their evening meal. As soon as Mum saw everyone start to go upstairs, she would often get agitated and immediately want to be taken upstairs too, even though the meal wasn't for another 30 minutes and she hadn't yet finished her tea and cake. She would be afraid that she would miss the meal, or there wasn't going to be a seat for her if she didn't go straightaway. It's tough dealing with 'irrational' anxiety, but I've learned to accept that her anxiety was real to her and that I needed to be responsive to her, if for no other reason that I could easily find myself sitting on my own downstairs like a numpty as she went upstairs to assuage her own anxiety!

3. Finding Emotional Maturity

As I've mentioned, my experience with Mum and her dementia has been a heck of a journey, during which I've transitioned from being the son to becoming the grown-up in our relationship. Parenting our parents can be a big deal. It is an initiation, crossing a threshold, realising that 'I am the grown-up now'. I am now at the front of the line, with no more parents to defer to. Many people cross this threshold when they themselves become parents, but not having had my own children, this journey with Mum has been my initiation.

Taking responsibility for our experiences

I have experienced a lot of despair, helplessness and guilt in life. I have been tough on myself, much tougher on myself than anyone else would ever be. But these are my experiences, as similar experiences might well be yours. When Mum first had dementia, and I hadn't really understood it, I blamed her for feeling difficult and being irritating. I felt victimised by her and her behaviour, but gradually came to understand that she was not doing this 'to me'; I was simply on the receiving end of her behaviour, as we all are on the receiving end of the behaviours of those we love, whether this is intended or not. However, in trying not to blame Mum or someone else, I have often ended up blaming myself.

I have needed to undergo a deep acceptance of these being my feelings and this being my experience. And to acknowledge that the greatest pressure has been the pressure I have put myself under, rather than any pressure anyone else has put on me.

4. Increase Your Willingness to Take Responsibility

For me, one of the gifts of this journey with my mum has been to develop and expand my relationship with the concept of responsibility. When I was young, I felt emotionally responsible for Mum. It felt like a heavy weight, and in retrospect, as a child, I clearly didn't have much faith in myself or confidence in my abilities to accept such a grown-up responsibility. I had a lot of fear around responsibility, seeing it as most likely an opportunity to get things wrong and screw up and get blamed. So I held myself back a lot, to avoid messing up.

Taking on Power of Attorney for Mum has been an initiation into having more faith in myself to make good decisions, and to get things 'right'. For me, there have been three key elements:

1. *Practical responsibility*: taking legal and practical responsibility for my mum and being in charge of her finances, health and well-being. Acting on her behalf as a landlord for her tenants.
2. *Being the responsible grown-up*: this is a major transition and involves an evolution of roles, a growth in maturity, and being the parent to the parent and taking responsibility for my mother.
3. *Taking responsibility for my own experience – emotional maturity:* accepting and acknowledging my experience and emotions on this journey.

Responsibility for Mum's well-being and finances

By the middle of 2019, Mum had been in the care home for approaching six years. I had been responsible for spending around £300,000 of her money on care-home fees and other expenses. I have also looked after her income from pensions and rent. I have been safeguarding her financial well-being. Safeguarding her care. Acting as her tenants' landlord. Dealing with the care home. Dealing with her tax. And walking with her as the disease has got progressively worse. I have safeguarded an inheritance for my sister and myself.

It's been a big responsibility, a real burden at times, partly because of the nature of the decisions themselves, and also the weight of being the one who has taken responsibility for making those decisions.

As I've mentioned, when I was growing up, there seemed a lot of blame in my family. I felt blamed for getting things wrong, and upsetting and disappointing people. As a grown-up, I now see this as being part of a dysfunctional upbringing, where family members were quick to blame each other, without taking responsibility for their own feelings and experiences. One of the biggest elements of my journey has been the willingness to give up blame.

I have at times been scared that I am not making the best decisions for Mum's well-being, that I am adding to her suffering rather than supporting her. It is a tough journey to be on even if you have a loving family behind you. I carried an old belief that I was inadequate, not enough of a man to cope; so one of the gifts of this journey has been to see more clearly how resourceful I can be and how much I am able to cope with. It has helped me expand my overall confidence in myself.

5. Grieving well

Visiting the care home on average once a week for nearly six years means that it has become a place of belonging for me too. I have got to know staff, residents and families. Many staff have come and gone over that period, many residents have died, and relatives I'd got to know no longer need to visit. Mum is now one of the people who has been there the longest.

Losing someone to dementia is not an event, but a process

Dementia can be like taking part in a marathon, but you have no idea how many miles you need to run, and no idea where the finishing line is. It is a long goodbye. You lose your loved one a memory at a time, each loss of recognition at a time, each day at a time. But because they are still there physically, I guess there is always the hidden hope that they might just come back. That they are just going through a bad patch. They have a good and lucid day – and there's the faint glimmer that everything will be OK again. Because they are still physically alive.

But with dementia, there isn't a dead body to grieve over; our loved ones are still alive. I found myself needing to do regular 'reality checks' with myself, often through talking to other people. I needed to keep reminding myself of the 'reality' of the situation with Mum. It's all too easy to go off into fantasies and imaginings.

Now that Mum and I have no memories to share together, no shared history, in many ways she is more of a stranger. She has few memories of her past, my past, her husband/my dad, her family. She is the woman who was my mother, rather than who is my mother.

One evening, after I left Mum and went to go to the Magic Wok for my Singapore noodles, I was feeling particularly sad, although I wasn't sure why. So I asked myself what I was so upset about. This is what came to me, and I realised it was a cumulative sadness, hitting me all at once:

- I was sad for Mum and her suffering.
- I felt sad for my ongoing loss.

- I was sad about the unfulfilled wish that she might see how much I loved her.
- I was sad for how helpless I felt at helping her feel good about herself.
- I was crying for the hope that she might recover and become fully lucid.
- I was crying that she would never be the mum I had always wanted and that she never quite was.
- I was crying for the other residents that I had become close to and loved over the years Mum had been there, and who'd loved me, and who had already died.
- I was sad when I looked at the sign in the care home's reception that said who had passed this week – knowing that one day it would be Mum's name there.
- I was sad to know that one day Mum would be gone and I would have no reason to visit anymore, and that slice of my life – the community, meaning and connection I had created at the care home – would have come to an end.
- I was crying for how alone I felt and the lack of support I sometimes felt – and that I don't have much family to talk to and be on this journey with.
- I was crying for the weight of responsibility I felt and the worry about whether I was doing OK, fearful of being criticised for what I was doing or not doing.
- I was crying out for someone to tell me what a job good I was doing and how proud of me they were and how much they admired the way I was handling things for Mum and myself.

I felt I had so much to be sad about, it seemed almost unbearable. Like too many of us, I tend to feel ashamed of sadness and keep it to myself, rather than ask for support.

Loss of identity and my role as a good son

Over the first year or two of Mum's time in the care home, I noticed that I was starting to feel a little less useful, at times even a little useless. Part of my identity had been that of a 'good and caring son' when she was still living at her old home. I was the son who took my mum shopping, cut her lawns, did basic DIY for her, kept her company, watched TV with her, encouraged her and did what I could to care about her and for her. These things gave me a sense of purpose and another reason for being. I had to grieve the loss of these roles too and the meaning they gave me. I had to discover who I was without those roles.

I felt I had become a little bit redundant, because the care home took over the caring. There had been things for me to do: clear her house, rent it out, look after her money, have meetings at the care home, but she didn't even realise I was doing most of them for her. I was no longer doing them for the reward of appreciation from her. And when those early jobs were largely completed, there were even fewer roles for me to play. I have had to grieve for the loss of my roles and the meaning, identity and purpose they once gave me.

It sounds obvious, but I have increasingly made my peace with the fact that there is nothing I can do or that can be done medically to reverse Mum's dementia. What I can do is to love her anyway. I don't have to feel so bad about feeling helpless. It's a fact. We are all largely helpless in some areas, while being potent in others.

I used to feel it was my job to stop Mum feeling bad about herself. My own liberation has been through realising that the 'jobs' I believed I had were those that I'd assigned myself. I don't think Mum had any sense that I had failed her, or that I had failed to save her from herself. I don't think she ever really gave me that role.

6. Handling guilt

My capacity to feel bad about myself can, it seems, sometimes know no bounds! I feel I could win a gold medal in feeling bad. I am not convinced that we are born guilty; I think we learn it. And I was taught a lot about guilt in my family. I used to think I had special Methodist form of guilt, but I have come to see that all guilt is the same – I don't think Methodist, Jewish, Hindu, Catholic or Muslim guilt are any different. It all feels horrible! And even worse, it has no real value, and it doesn't make anything better.

A big question for me when Mum first went into the home was wondering whether I was forcing her into some hellish experience, keeping her somewhere she didn't want to be. That was something to feel really guilty about!

I think Mum believed she needed someone to rescue her from her own suffering, and, as I've mentioned, for a lot of my life I had tried to rescue her. While, of course, it was impossible for me to do that, it didn't stop me trying and regularly feeling guilty that I couldn't succeed. I had some grandiose belief that I should be able to have the power to rescue her – but then felt a failure for not being able to.

Inevitably perhaps, Mum's dementia has given me plenty of opportunities to feel guilty and bad about myself. So, in a painful way, at first it was like a toxic gift because I couldn't escape seeing my guilt. It was there and I couldn't deny it. I felt like I was trapped in it, almost addicted to it.

Guilt is prevalent

I think guilt is one of the key feelings many people have around a loved one with dementia. I can understand why some people simply withdraw and don't go to see their loved one if they don't live with them. While withdrawal is one way of coping with guilt, it doesn't make it go away, although it can seem to keep it at bay.

I felt guilty that I haven't become a full-time carer and laid down my life for Mum! It's easy to feel guilty for not being willing or able to do more. There is always more you think you could do or should have done. My harsh inner critic can have a field day.

Project it out

Another way of handling our guilt can be to bury it and project it onto others – by making them the guilty ones, so we can keep our own guilt a little further at bay. The days after I had the 85 phone calls from Mum, for instance, I wanted to make the care home the guilty ones. Blame them. Make them wrong.

Guilt about our own needs

I also felt guilty about needing things for myself and caring for myself, as I had a deep training in self-martyrdom. At times, when I was growing up, I even felt that I was wrong to exist. So I tried to shrink myself and not take up too much space. I tried not to be a nuisance or need anything for myself. I believed I shouldn't think about myself. This approach has brought me close to burnout several times in my life, including during the period while Mum has been in the care home.

I have believed that I am only OK when I am somehow relieving other people's suffering, often at great personal expense to myself. There is still that little boy in me who felt he had to relieve his mother's pain and who has been trying to do so ever since, while also believing that he was failing. As a child, I even thought that I was supposed to give up my own life to help Mum – Mum came from a generation who believed they had to sacrifice their own needs for their children and family, and I felt I was supposed to do the same.

On a good day, when Mum and I have really connected, she may plead with me not to leave her on her own at the home, and ask that I stay there with her. I still hate the white lie of telling her that I will be back in a while when I know I will be going home.

I am still taming my own guilt and continuing to get a handle on it…

Trying to pay off the guilt

Because I have felt so guilty, I have tried at times very hard to pay off my guilt, usually through making myself suffer in some way. Through sacrifice, through people pleasing, by ignoring my own needs and self-care, I've hoped to assuage the guilty voices in my head. Another way I've tried to pay off guilt has been by punishing myself and caring about everyone else but not really looking after myself.

I think we can also feel guilty about how angry and resentful we can feel at times in relation to a loved one with dementia. Guilty about the time and energy we have to invest in caring, rather than enjoying the process or it being our pleasure. Mum would probably enjoy having me visit every day – although she wouldn't realise that I was! A 90-minute visit to see her can take me seven hours in total. If I lived around the corner, I would visit more often, but I now realise that if I miss a week, she doesn't have much concept of time, and won't berate me. I would probably berate myself, though.

At other times it can feel like a privilege to care, yet guilt nevertheless distorts so much of our thinking, feeling and understanding of what is real. So a surprising gift of this journey has been firstly to bring all this guilt to the surface, which hasn't been very pleasant, but then to see through it and find my 'innocence' and my 'enoughness' again. Crazy as it sounds, one of the gifts of dementia has been to expose so much of my hidden guilt that I can recognise it for what it is – and let it go. Even today, though, when mum asks if I have come to take her home, I still find it hard to say, "No, I haven't. This is where you live now."

7. Caring for Yourself

One of the hardest and most needed lessons for me has been around caring for myself. I enjoy giving from a place of fullness but have often felt that my own well has run dry, and I've just kept pushing myself all the same. I've found it hard to stop and care about myself and renew myself. I've felt guilty if I do.

As I've explained, I grew up believing that my job was to care for everyone else. I operated from a sense of duty, putting others first, and I learned to sacrifice my own needs. My value derived from what I did for others. I tried as hard as I could not to need anything for myself, believing I was selfish if I did. I actually felt ashamed of needing anything for myself. I believed I shouldn't need anything, and not give to myself, care about myself or care for myself. The idea was that good people don't need anything for themselves. It's holy to give and selfish to receive.

It might be clear by now that martyrdom and self-sacrifice ran deep in my family, and were seen as a virtue. I think we believed that if we suffered enough, then happiness might be the reward. So I learned to cover up all my problems, weaknesses and vulnerabilities. To put a lid on everything. I hated my own needs and wants, believing they made me weak.

You don't need to be a rocket scientist to figure out that this mindset often hasn't turned out well for me. I burn out. I get exhausted. I get cranky and resentful. I can come to a full stop and feel empty. When I take a week off from visiting Mum, I can still feel guilt ridden, even when I have been ill.

So a gift for me in this journey has been to learn to take better care of myself. To understand and acknowledge my own needs, and not to be ashamed of having them. And to be kind and compassionate to myself. It hasn't come naturally for me to see myself as worthwhile, valuable and significance. I have found it easier to give and uncomfortable to feel like I sometimes have to receive.

What is 'enough' caring?

Part of self-care is about having clear boundaries around what 'enough' is – and I haven't found this easy.

- What are my boundaries?
- How do I decide what is enough caring?
- How do I set boundaries?
- How do I handle critics or, more importantly, my own inner critic which says I should be doing more?
- And what would more caring even look like?

There are no clear answers, no magic manual in which to look up the answers. These are questions we all have to navigate for ourselves. In some ways, I felt I could never do enough for Mum, and that I failed to meet her needs, but I now understand that it never was my job to meet her needs. So much comes down to our own moods, and how resourceful we are feeling in any moment. More knowledge and calmer times can result in different perceptions.

8. The skill of drawing out the essence of our loved one

Part of understanding how to have as good a relationship as possible with our loved one with dementia is to see that what shows on the surface is only the tip of the iceberg. Aspects of the person are still in there and reappear in certain circumstances; such as when Gary, the Elvis impersonator, comes to visit and residents start dancing and singing along. When the activities team put on a CD of songs that were popular around the Second World War, many residents come to life, and remember amazing things. Likewise, when children from a local dance school came in to perform, a lot of the residents became very animated and responsive. I was also amazed at the response when they brought in a Shetland pony, a cat and an owl to meet the residents.

One day I found Mum holding a doll, and it seemed to connect her with happy memories of being a mother and to draw out something lovely in her. So I ordered a doll like it on Amazon and when she held it, it seemed to both calm her and make her happy, at least for a few moments. And at other times, the doll didn't seem to register with her at all.

After one visit, Kaye, the home manager, gave me a lift to the station, and told me a story about one of the other residents. She said the resident didn't speak much at all, and then one day, he suddenly became lucid for several hours. He talked about his life, how he had been a Spitfire pilot. His daughter was there, and they had an amazing conversation before he withdrew back in to himself again.

Several times, I have witnessed Mum sitting in a withdrawn state in the lounge, and then I have picked up one of the beach balls that are sometimes in there and thrown it to her, and suddenly she and the other residents have come to life for a few moments. Somehow the beach ball 'reaches' a part of them that is still in there, but needs to be nurtured, encouraged and stimulated, and drawn out in some way. Something needs to be unlocked, and we may be able to find the key to enable that.

Irma, the activities manager, knows that it would be wonderful to have a Sensory Room at the home. These rooms are designed to calm residents down so their anxiety is alleviated and they are more 'accessible'. The rooms cost around £50,000 to kit out, so she is fundraising to get one built.

I often find that simply holding hands with Mum, smiling at her and giving her compliments is the best way to draw her out. But it's not always easy or even possible to connect in this way. It takes time, patience and a willingness to engage, to try things and learn. What works one day may not work another day. Other times, when I have held her hand, she has been unpleasant and told me to leave.

A significant part of my work as a coach, writer and speaker is informed by the belief that there are skills, gifts, abilities and capabilities dormant or latent within each of us, and to help people draw these out. We may be aware that they are there, and need support to access them, so that they can be 'discovered'. So I try to do this with Mum too; sometimes it works, other times it doesn't, and to be honest, sometimes I am simply worn out and don't have the bandwidth to do it.

You are not your thoughts and feelings

One of the most liberating gifts of this journey has been to expand and evolve my relationship with my thoughts and feelings. Mostly, we associate ourselves *with* our thoughts and feelings. We can easily think that we *are* our thoughts and feelings. However, it is really helpful to create a little more distance from our emotions and to become the observer of our thoughts and feelings, rather than being totally immersed in them. We are the person who *experiences* our thoughts and feelings, but not the thoughts and feelings themselves.

An area where I have found this idea especially helpful is around the idea of cruelty.

Dementia is frequently described as a cruel disease because of the effects it has on our loved one, because of the ways they change, and the change in our relationship with them. There can also be other elements concerning cruelty:

We may have concerns that carers may be cruel to our loved one – we want to know our loved ones are safe and don't experience abuse.

Because of the changes in their brain structure and brain chemistry, a loved one with dementia can appear to act towards us in ways that can feel cruel. They can, for instance, appear nasty when they are acting out of fear, frustration and confusion.

Their ongoing dementia can also trigger some of our own cruel thoughts. We might find ourselves thinking: How much longer are they going to live? Is there going to be any of my inheritance left after all these care-home fees? Why have I had to give up so much of my life for them?

I think we often keep our own cruel thoughts secret because we feel ashamed of having them. We feel guilty. If we think we are our thoughts, then we believe that our thoughts shape our identity (although, as we have seen, our thoughts do not constitute our identity). When we have cruel or nasty thoughts, we can believe these make us a cruel or nasty person. And if we aren't comfortable with those thoughts, we can easily try to compensate or even over-compensate for how horrible we think we might be, by trying to be an even better partner, child or friend, to prove we are not the horrible person we fear we are.

However, having a few cruel thoughts doesn't necessarily make us bad people. I think it is important that we let ourselves have all of our thoughts and feelings – obviously not to act them out, but not to judge or suppress them either. And when we can, we should share them with people who we know will not be judgemental of us, but who will be understanding.

Paradoxically, the more we try to resist and judge our thoughts and feelings, the stronger they might become. And they might burst out in inappropriate ways. Simply noticing them and allowing them to exist without judgement can be very powerful. This approach is often called mindfulness, meaning that we simply notice our thoughts and feelings, without associating ourselves with them too closely. They are your thoughts, but they are not you. You are not your thoughts.

9. Handling the family dynamics

I have left this section to next to last, because it is an area where I feel like I am still on the nursery slopes of understanding. Firstly, I don't have much family – there is my partner Helen, and my sister Amanda, but no children, all my aunts and uncles are dead, no nephews or nieces, and some cousins I occasionally see. I share LPA (Lasting Power of Attorney) with my cousin Peter, and that is because when Mum was of a sounder mind, she asked both my sister and I to act as LPA when the time came. However, my sister refused to act as LPA with me, so after an almighty tussle, she declined to sign the papers that were drawn up, and my cousin stepped in to act as a back-up.

I know from friends and family that the experiences of parental bereavement, or caring for someone with an illness like dementia, can open up a can of worms when it comes to family dynamics, releasing unresolved feelings that have been under the surface but which have been manageable until now. Things can either be resolved and hopefully draw people closer together, or things can get blown apart.

All the 'who cares most', the guilt, those sibling rivalries from decades earlier, and feelings about the unfair sharing of responsibilities can spill out. I've seen other fragile sibling relationships pushed over the precipice through the stress.

Amanda and I have such different ways of looking at things. When my dad was still alive, we rallied around him and for him, but when he died, it was a little like the heart of the family that had kept us together had been ripped out.

I have always had a strong motivation to please, but when it came to dealing my mum's dementia, I realised I now needed to be fierce in a way that didn't come naturally to me, in order to do things that I thought were in Mum's best interests, but which Amanda wasn't necessarily happy about. I sensed that her gripe was with me personally rather than with what I was actually doing. Understandably, we fought a lot. Things got worse and we are now completely estranged. As a result, I have chosen to exclude her from my life and I only communicate with her about when I am visiting Mum.

But the gift for me in this family situation has been about getting to know and appreciate myself, to see my own positive qualities, to learn to set my own clear boundaries. I can still find it hard not blame myself for things that are not my responsibility. I am still learning to recognise that my clear boundaries can be the trigger for someone else's upset, but their upset doesn't mean I shouldn't set boundaries. I understand now that when I don't please people, I am not 'bad'. I aim increasingly to keep my main goal in mind and to be effective in pursuit of it: Mum's well-being and the most comfortable end of life she can have.

10. Beyond emotional inheritance

I resonate with the idea that we inherit and pass on emotions, ideas and patterns from person to person, from generation to generation. I like the idea that we are all a mash-up of biology, ancestry and mystery. I am a product of my ancestry, as we all are.

I feel like I inherited a lot from Mum. Some great qualities, such as loyalty, a genuine and positive stoicism, manners, and a sense of duty towards others. However, I've also inherited ideas that haven't served me so well. Mum was born in 1930, and grew up during the Second World War. She was one of eight children growing up in a two-bedroom house in Staines, with an outside toilet. There was a factory at the bottom of her garden that was a target for German bombing, so she grew up with bombs dropping and regular visits to the air-raid shelters. I doubt she knew much nurturing herself; she grew up with a lot of anxiety and has always been quite an anxious person. I have similarly experienced a lot of anxiety during the course of my life.

Life was quite austere for her and her family. I think there was some abuse. She simply had to endure things; there was no point in trying to change anything. She had to get on with things doggedly, regardless of how she might have felt. I expect aspects of her life were hell. She seemed to have a belief that life is tough and often hard, and you are powerless to do anything about it, so you have to try to get through it however you can. You simply have to endure suffering. You have to be strong to survive and can't afford the luxury of showing any weakness, and shouldn't expect too much joy.

I am guessing that owing to a combination of her upbringing and Christian beliefs, Mum prided herself on not needing a lot and depriving herself; she didn't want much, need much or ask for much. Through her, I think I learned that good people 'should' deprive themselves. And that bad people were selfish and looked out for themselves. My emotional needs were just a nuisance, and I learned to judge myself as weak for even having them. I tried to be a good person – a good Christian, as I understood that to be – but it certainly didn't make me happy; quite the opposite. My inner impulse was always to be fully myself, even though I tried really hard to be who I thought I should be.

Even though I didn't grow up in the 1930s and 40s, I felt like I'd inherited many of those emotions and patterns. Her beliefs and feelings seemed to live on within me, just as she may well have inherited them from her ancestors. I felt a need to endure difficulties and suffering, and not try to make things too much better for myself.

So another gift of this journey has been to help me identify this emotional inheritance, and to sort and sift through it, and become freer of it. To give myself an emotional reboot and gradually begin to free myself of it, updating the operating system of my own mind. I have brought my own thinking and emotions up to date, so that more of the time I am living my own authentic life, rather than the script I was handed down by my forebears. I don't think I knew until I embarked on this journey with Mum quite how conditioned I had become or how much there was going to be to undo.

CONCLUSION

This journey with Mum has really tested who I've felt myself to be, and at the same time helped reveal more of who I really am. Very few diseases test the people around the one with the disease in the way that dementia does. I have come to realise that there is nothing wrong with me for finding this experience difficult. Most people don't breeze through this journey. We all struggle. We all wonder whether there is some insight or magic trick we might be able to find to make things easier. Ever since I was a child I've thought I should be able to stop bad things happening to the people I care about, but now I know that however much I might want to, I can't.

I know I only have one shot at this time with Mum, so I have tried to make it a precious journey, despite all the difficulties. Increasingly now, when I ask myself whether there is anything more I could or should have done for Mum, I accept that the reality is, given the circumstances, no, not really. While I've known that for some time intellectually, I am now allowing myself to feel it. Amanda didn't want to become a full-time carer, and neither did Helen and I. And given that Mum can no longer care for herself, the options were either full-time care in her own home or a care home. All the professional and personal advice I sought pointed to a care home being the best option for Mum.

I have wanted to go through this experience with Mum as gracefully and authentically as I can. I started off alone, a little clueless and all at sea. It's a hard journey and I have wanted to do my best to avoid regrets when Mum dies. At the end of it, I want to be as sure as I can be that I did what was necessary and gave Mum the best care she could have had. I've dreaded the possibility that after she has dies, I would then discover something that I wish I'd known while she was alive that would have made a difference.

I think one of the hardest things is not being able to relieve the suffering of the people we care about. Dementia faces us with our loved one's suffering, and often there is not a lot we can do to alleviate it. It asks us to face our limits: what we are willing to do and which sacrifices we are not willing to make. But we don't have to feel bad, guilty or that we are a failure. As a man, I like to be the hero, to fix things and solve problems. It has been hard for me to accept that I can't do this with my mum and her dementia. I don't have a cure for dementia, but I can be a loving and kind witness and companion to my mum.

I am clear now that it is tough, if not impossible, to get through this alone. You are forced, in a good way, to open up, to ask for and get support, to let people in.

What is my perspective on emotional maturity now?

I have had three decades of consciously adventuring and pioneering in my life. These decades have taken me from a safe corporate job to starting my own business, and becoming a speaker and a coach. To starting a long-term relationship with Helen. Then entering the world of writing and becoming an author, getting to speak around the world. Becoming an authority in my area, and being hired by some amazing leaders and companies. Dealing with Dad's decline and death. And for the last six years, venturing with Mum into the world of dementia.

Each chapter in this book has stirred up lots of fear, anxiety and resistance in me – as well as hope, inspiration and a sense of fulfilment. While I am no stranger to the extremes of my feelings, as I have explained, I have often experienced a lot of shame around them, seeing them as weaknesses rather than strengths. I have judged myself as 'over-sensitive' and unable to cope easily with what others seem to breeze through. I can easily feel temporarily overwhelmed by my emotions, and sometimes feel barely able to function because I can get so upset. I often wish I could just 'be strong' rather than have all these emotions. These last six years with Mum and her dementia have offered me a massive opportunity to experience and make friends with my feelings.

In a funny and painful way, this journey has done wonders for my sense of self-confidence. It has meant that I have had to rebuild my sense of inner validation. From having felt so bad about myself in the past, I now feel better about myself than I have done maybe for my whole life. I have developed for myself an inner 'good parent' that validates me and sees the good in me. I no longer see myself as a bad person. I have become a better parent to myself than I have ever been. I also think I have found a link between parenting and my fascination with great leadership – and I think leadership, and what we would like to receive from our leaders, has a lot to do with our own parenting experiences.

The bigger opportunity – greater awareness and skills around dementia

Even though I have had this immersion in the world of dementia, I still feel like a bit of a novice. Most of us don't get any exposure to it, or any training in it, before we are faced with the dementia of those we love. I still feel strongly that I would love to see care homes offering emotional support for the families of loved ones with dementia as a matter of course. And I am happy to see that awareness of dementia is increasing. I know my initial reactions were often fearful, and I can understand that people needing to deal with those with dementia in any public field would feel similarly unskilled and potentially afraid.

My friend Jane is one of the people who nudged me to write this book. Her own mother has dementia, and she recently attended a conference on the subject. She heard that there are currently well over 4,500 people in her local area alone who have been diagnosed with dementia (let alone those with undiagnosed dementia), but there only two Admiral Nurses to support them. (Admiral Nurses provide the specialist dementia support that families need.) Two nurses for all those families!

There is a ton of information available online about dementia and Alzheimer's, but there are fewer experienced people who are both willing and able to guide us. I know it's not that care homes don't care, but their legitimate focus is on the needs of their residents, rather than the families of the residents. Personally, I was lucky that my mother's care home had Irma Aleshe at the helm and I struck up a friendship with her. I was able to acknowledge my own struggles and specifically asked for help; otherwise I probably wouldn't have got it. At the time, I didn't even really know what I needed, so would have found it hard to know what to ask for. In the appendix, you will find the booklet that Irma and I co-authored as a result of our conversations.

I believe the invitation and opportunity are there for us to guide each other, share what we learn as we go, and to offer each other peer support – and to be friends helping friends, all on this journey together.

DEMENTIA AND ALZHEIMER'S
BASIC ROAD MAP TO NURTURING YOUR LOVED ONE

(also applicable to the anxiety-prone and people with memory-loss episodes)

by Irma Aleshe and Nick Williams

ROAD JUNCTION: dementia in plain terms

What's going on..?

Dementia is a progressive deterioration of the brain's function. The brain starts to reverse on itself. The natural neural pathways to brain processes begin to get blocked. This then interferes with different functions, depending on which pathways are affected, thus inhibiting and removing basic functions, viz: forgetfulness, short-term memory loss, problems with face recognition and object identification, impaired mental capacity, elevated aggression, difficulties with cognitive reasoning, difficult mobility, social inhibitions drop away, inappropriate speech and behaviour, and more.

Simply put, expressions rear up that are in total conflict with your recollection of your loved one's persona.

TRAFFIC LIGHTS: internal workings, points of note

Each person experiences dementia in ways unique to them, but some similar traits occur across the spectrum:

- Individuals with dementia can feel trapped in their own mind and body, and unable to effectively express or verbalise themselves to others.
- When their attempts at communication are misread or ignored, this can provoke fear, frustration, panic and anxiety, which may lead to lashing out or aggressiveness.
- Individuals with dementia are not to be treated in a condescending manner: even though their actions can be 'childlike', they are certainly not children and are very well tuned in to emotions.
- In certain instances, prescribed medication has been helpful in moderating anxiety and aggressiveness.
- Individuals might not recall having had a very recent meal/activity, but can display amazing clarity and accuracy recounting events from their childhood/teen/young adult lives.

ROAD BUMPS: do these sound familiar…?
'I want to go home / take me home now!'
'I hate being a nuisance / I know I am a nuisance!'
'I just want to die!'
'I haven't had my tablets/breakfast /lunch!'
'Why am I here..?!'
…spontaneous tears…
'Where is [insert dead spouse's name]?'
'Why aren't they here? / Where have they gone..?' and more…

- The same question repeated over and again, till it may make you feel quite pressured and/or frustrated.

- Utterances and statements that do not make 'sense', or which have no apparent bearing on the person's current activity.

THE ROAD SIGNS: negative triggers

Avoid the following dead-ends:

- Trying to reason with them over a statement that does not make sense.
- Attempting to make them think more clearly.
- Telling them they are wrong.
- Expressing your frustration to them.
- Saying that *they* don't understand.
- Not listening or paying them attention when they are in need.
- Correcting their speech.
- Belittling their words or being condescending.

DIVERSIONS: learning to relate better

Take the following nurturing pathways:

- In every instance, be very empathetic, validate and honour their feelings.
- Flow along with every train of thought and distract them with positive suggestions.
- Be demonstrably affectionate and loving to them: hold hands, offer hugs and kisses, stroke their arm/hair/face, smile lots, laugh with them, be free with compliments, and celebrate them.
- Engage in fun pastimes, such as games and puzzles, walks, music, reading books and newspapers,

looking at family photos and videos, art and other creative activities.

- Reminisce about happy memories.
- Where possible and appropriate, assist them in personal and social care, such as eating, dressing, and such like.
- Be sensitive and aware of their moods; for instance, a tired relative is better left to rest.

STOP LIGHTS: you matter too – recognising and handling your feelings

Dealing with a loved one who's experiencing dementia can be a tough, long and strange journey. Being aware of, and taking care of your feelings, are vital to coping with the changes.

- It is important to acknowledge rather than try to deny your feelings.
- Build a support base by talking to people (such as doctors, nurses, care professionals) who understand the process and have the compassion and skill to walk you through your journey. Join a local dementia group, as sharing with people on a similar journey can be very uplifting and offer practical insights.
- Treasure the moments of happiness, laughter and joy that you have with your loved one. Find a balance and don't focus on the difficult episodes.
- Try journaling to make sense of your experiences, thoughts and feelings.
- Join in activities with your relative when they are up and having their happier times. Witness and

share with them in moments of enjoyment.

- Painful as the journey may be, humour is very therapeutic and developing more of this sense will ease the burden of care.

Final note

Leave the very tough bits to the professionals. They care and can cope better than you may be able to do, because they do not carry the guilt of an emotional connection.

RESOURCES

Irma Aleshe, e-mail: **yaboh@aol.com**

Age UK: **www.ageuk.org.uk/information-advice/health-wellbeing/conditions-illnesses/dementia/getting-care-and-support**

Alzheimer's Society: **www.alzheimers.org.uk**

Alzheimer's Society Blog: **www.alzheimers.org.uk/blog/lying-to-somebody-with-dementia**

Dementia UK : **www.dementiauk.org**

NHS: **www.nhs.uk/conditions/dementia/help-and-support**

STAY IN TOUCH

I live in Finchley, North London. Professionally, I teach, coach and guide inspirational leaders around the world, in person and online. I also give key-note talks on inspirational leadership at conferences and in companies.

As I've mentioned in this book, I am not an expert on dementia, but if I can help in any way, please do drop me line.

My website is: **www.iamnickwilliams.com**

You can contact me on: **nick@iamnickwilliams.com**

You can connect with me at:
www.linkedin.com/in/nickwilliamsauthor
www.facebook.com/nickwilliamsauthor

I am on Twitter: **@nickwilliams1**

Read peer praise:
www.iamnickwilliams.com/about/peer-feedback

Learn more about my speaking experience:
www.iamnickwilliams.com/signature-work/keynote-speaking

Find out more about my media experience:
www.iamnickwilliams.com/about/media

Printed in Great Britain
by Amazon

63848018R00052